The
Listening
Walk

The Listening

Walk

by PAUL SHOWERS
illustrated by ALIKI

35910

THOMAS Y. CROWELL COMPANY   New York

LET'S-READ-AND-FIND-OUT SCIENCE BOOKS

Editors: DR. ROMA GANS, Professor Emeritus of Childhood Education, Teachers College, Columbia University
DR. FRANKLYN M. BRANLEY, Astronomer Emeritus and former Chairman of The American Museum–Hayden Planetarium

AIR, WATER, AND WEATHER

Air Is All Around You
The Clean Brook
Flash, Crash, Rumble, and Roll
Floating and Sinking
Icebergs
North, South, East, and West
Oxygen Keeps You Alive
·Rain and Hail
Snow Is Falling
Sunshine Makes the Seasons
Water for Dinosaurs and You
Where the Brook Begins

THE EARTH AND ITS COMPOSITION

The Bottom of the Sea
Caves

Fossils Tell of Long Ago
Glaciers
A Map Is a Picture
Millions and Millions of Crystals
Oil: The Buried Treasure
Salt
Where Does the Garbage Go?
The Wonder of Stones

ASTRONOMY AND SPACE

The Beginning of the Earth
The Big Dipper
Eclipse: Darkness in Daytime
The Moon Seems to Change
Rockets and Satellites
The Sun: Our Nearest Star
What Makes Day and Night
What the Moon Is Like*

MATTER AND ENERGY

Energy from the Sun
Gravity Is a Mystery
High Sounds, Low Sounds
Hot as an Ice Cube
Light and Darkness
The Listening Walk
Streamlined
Upstairs and Downstairs
Weight and Weightlessness
What Makes a Shadow?

And other books on LIVING THINGS: PLANTS; LIVING THINGS: ANIMALS, BIRDS, FISH, INSECTS, ETC.; and THE HUMAN BODY

* Available in Spanish.

REC Library Edition reprinted with the permission of Thomas Y. Crowell Company

Responsive Environments Corp., Englewood Cliffs, N. J. 07632   L.C. Card 61-10495

ISBN 0-690-49662-1, 0-690-49663-X (LB)

5   6   7   8   9   10

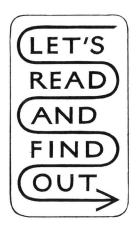

The
Listening
Walk

I like to take walks.

I take walks with my father and our dog.

Our dog is called Major.

He is an old dog and he does not walk very fast.

We go down the street and we do not talk.

My father puffs his pipe and thinks.

Major walks ahead and sniffs.

I keep still and listen.

I call this a Listening Walk.
On a Listening Walk I do not talk.
I listen to all the different sounds.
I hear many different sounds when I do not talk.

First I hear Major's toenails on the sidewalk.
Major is an old dog. He has long toenails.
When he walks, his toenails scratch the sidewalk.

They go *twick* *twick* *twick* *twick*.

I hear my father's shoes on the sidewalk.
My father walks slowly and his shoes go *dop* *dup* *dop* *dup*.

I can't hear my shoes. I wear sneakers.

I hear all sorts of sounds on a Listening Walk.
I listen to sounds I never listened to before.
I listen to lawn mowers.
Lawn mowers are noisy.

A power mower has a motor.
The motor makes a steady zooming noise.
It goes like this:

z-z-z-z-zzzzzzooooooooooooooooommmm.

A lawn mower that you push makes a different noise.
It goes

ratch   atch   atch   atch   atch.

If you push it faster, it makes more noise.
Like this:

ratch-atch-atch-atch-atch.

11

I like to listen to lawn sprinklers.
Lawn sprinklers are very quiet.
They make different sounds.
Some sprinklers make a steady whispering sound.
Like this:

thhhhhhhhhhhhhhhhhh.

Other sprinklers turn around and around.
They go like this:

whithhhhh   *whithhhhh*   *whithhhhh*   *whithhhhh.*

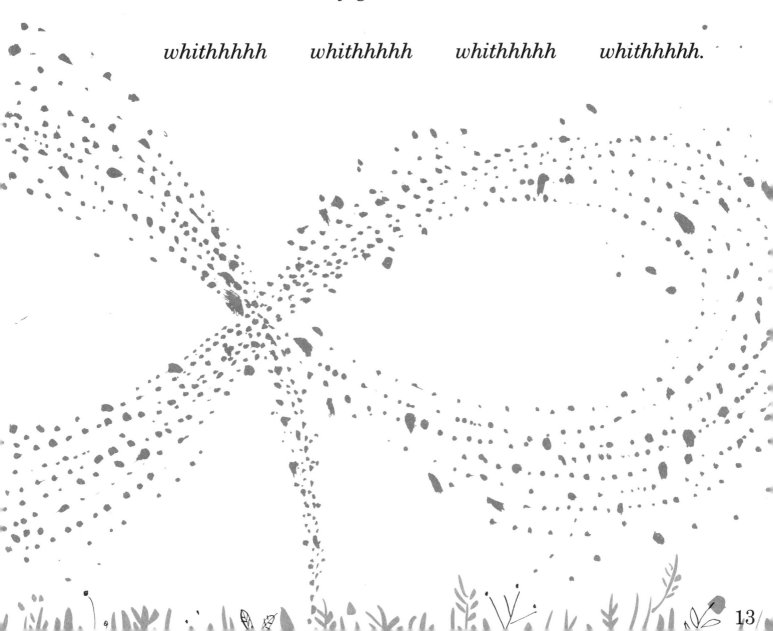

On a Listening Walk I hear cars in the street.

The shiny new cars are quiet.
They make only a soft *hmmmmmmmmmmmmmm.*

But old cars are very noisy.
Old cars sound like this:

rackety rack
rackety rack   *rackety rack.*

When cars stop quickly, the brakes go *eeeeeeeeeeeeeeeeeeee*.

the tires go *whhrrrrrrrrrrrr.*

On a Listening Walk I hear all kinds of sounds.

A baby crying:

waaaa   awaaaa   awaaaa   awaaaa.

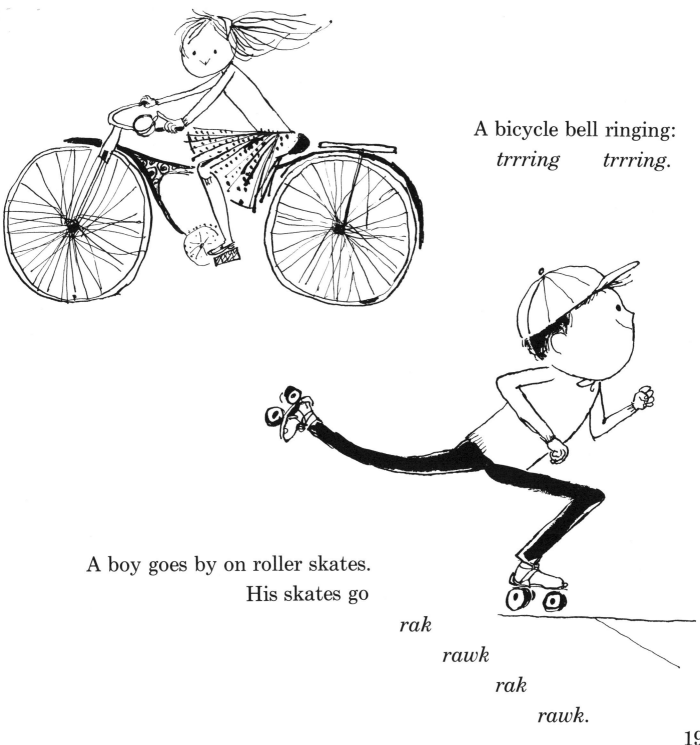

A bicycle bell ringing:
trrring   trrring.

A boy goes by on roller skates.
His skates go

rak

rawk

rak

rawk.

19

A lady hurries by us.
She is wearing high heels.
The lady's high heels go
    bik
       bok
          bik
            bok.

A bus is coming.
The lady starts to run:
    bik
       bik
          bik
            bik.

The bus stops at the corner:
  pfssssssss.
The lady gets on.

The bus starts up again:
  chrrrooooooooff.

21

Sometimes my father and I take Major to the park.

I like it in the park.

It is cool and shady.

It is quiet there until a jet flies over.

Jets are very noisy. A jet goes

eeeeeeeyowwwoooooooooooooo.

In the park my father and Major and I walk down the shady path.
I like to listen for sounds in the park.
They are not loud sounds like the noises in the street.
I have to keep very quiet to hear them.

We walk along the dirt path under the trees.
I do not talk. I listen.
I listen to my father's shoes on the path.
They make a soft sound. They go

chuff
  chuff
    chuff
      chuff.

I listen to the birds in the park.
I listen to the pigeons and the ducks.
The pigeons fly down to meet us.
They want us to feed them.

The pigeons puff up their feathers.
They take little, tiny steps.
They come toward us, nodding their heads.
They say

   prrrooo

       prrrooo   *prrrooo.*

      prrrooo

At the pond the ducks are waiting.
They want us to feed them, too.
The small ducks swim up close.
They turn their heads on one side and look at us.
The small ducks waggle their tails and quack.
The small ducks say

gank gank

wonk wonk

gank gank.

The big ducks are not so brave.
They stay back and swim around in circles.
The big ducks look at us but they do not come close.
The big ducks say

gaaaaank   *gaaaaank*   *gaaaaank.*

I like it in the park.

I hear many different sounds there.

I listen to the birds.

I hear the ducks and the pigeons.

Sometimes I hear a woodpecker.

The woodpecker sounds like a little hammer.

He goes

    rat-tat-tat-tat-tat-tat.

I hear many sounds in the park.

I hear crickets in the grass.

They go

    creet   creet   creet.

I hear the wind in the leaves.
It whispers

shhhhhhhhhhh.

I hear bees in the flowers:

bzzzzzzzzzzzzzzzzzzzzzzzzzzzz.

It is fun to go on a Listening Walk.
You do not have to go far.
You can walk around the block and listen.

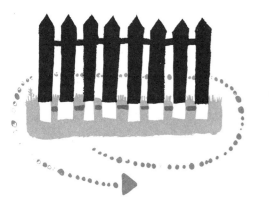

You can walk around your yard and listen.

You do not even have to take a walk to hear sounds.
There are sounds everywhere all the time.
All you have to do is to keep still and listen to them.
Right now there are sounds you can hear.